Icebergs

Contents

	page
The Ice Age	2
The Arctic Region	4
The Antarctic Region	6
Glaciers	8
Ice Shelves	9
Icebergs	10
Pack Ice	20
What if the Ice Melted?	22
Glossary	23
Index	24

The Ice Age

A long time ago, the world was very cold. Ice covered most of the land. This cold time lasted millions of years and was called an ice age. The last ice age ended around 12,000 years ago. The Earth slowly warmed up and much of the ice melted.

During the last ice age, much of the Earth looked like this.

Today ice has formed as ice caps and sheets, glaciers, icebergs and pack ice. Most of the ice occurs at the tips, or poles, of the Earth. These two regions are called the Arctic and the Antarctic.

The Arctic Region

The North Pole is in the Arctic region. Most of the Arctic region is ice-covered ocean. The northern parts of countries such as Russia, Canada and Norway are also in the Arctic region.

In the middle of the Arctic region is an enormous ice cap.

Animals and plants do live in the Arctic. Arctic mammals include hares, Arctic foxes, seals and polar bears. People, such as the Inuit and Lapps, live in the Arctic region.

The traditional costume of Lapps is warm and very colourful.

The Antarctic Region

The South Pole lies in the middle of a huge ice-covered continent called Antarctica. The very thick ice there is called an ice sheet. It is the coldest place on Earth.

The ice sheet that covers Antarctica contains 90% of the fresh water on Earth.

Fewer animals and plants live in the Antarctic than in the Arctic. Penguins, seals and some birds live there. The only people who live in the Antarctic are scientists who do research.

Emperor penguins

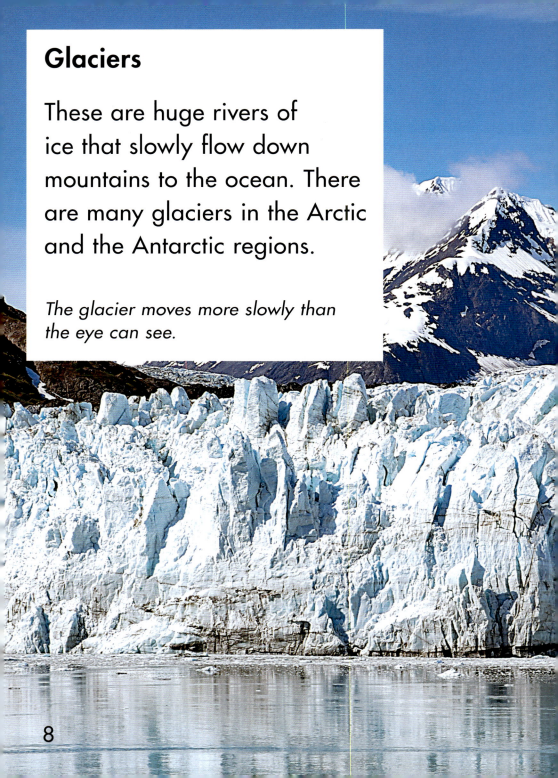

Glaciers

These are huge rivers of ice that slowly flow down mountains to the ocean. There are many glaciers in the Arctic and the Antarctic regions.

The glacier moves more slowly than the eye can see.

Ice Shelves

When the ice reaches the ocean, it keeps pushing out. It can make a huge floating ice shelf on the water.

The largest ice shelf is the Ross Ice Shelf in Antarctica.

Icebergs

Sometimes, a big chunk of ice breaks off from an ice shelf. It falls rumbling into the ocean and floats away. This is an iceberg.

An iceberg may look small, but it is actually very big. Only a small part of it can be seen above the water. Most of the iceberg is underwater, out of sight.

Between one-seventh and one-tenth of an iceberg can be seen above the water. This makes it dangerous to shipping.

Some icebergs, especially in the Antarctic, can be gigantic. In March 2000, an iceberg named B15 broke away from an ice shelf in Antarctica. It was 295 kilometres long and covered an area six times the size of Greater London.

Smaller parts of B15 were still being tracked after it broke away from the ice shelf. Those parts have since melted as the icebergs moved into warmer water.

Icebergs begin melting as soon as they break away from an ice shelf or glacier. They melt slowly.

This satellite photo shows a small part of B15 floating off the coast of Antarctica 13 years after it broke away.

Icebergs can be very dangerous. In 1912, a large passenger ship called the Titanic was sailing from England to New York when it hit an iceberg in the North Atlantic Ocean. It sank to the bottom of the ocean.

When the Titanic sank, 1,500 people drowned.

Today, scientists mainly use radar and satellite images to track the paths of icebergs. Sometimes ships such as this icebreaker work with helicopters or drones on iceberg patrols. They make sure that there are no icebergs around that can endanger passing ships.

Helicopters fly out over the sea and plot the positions of all the icebergs they can find.

As an iceberg floats along, the wind and the weather can carve the ice into strange shapes.

Icebergs are made of fresh water. Some scientists and engineers believe that one day it will be possible to tow them to provide drinking water for dry parts of the world.

Tugboats are able to move small icebergs when necessary. But before large icebergs can be used as sources of water, people must solve the problem of how to move them.

Pack Ice

In the polar regions, sea water freezes into big sheets of ice in the winter. This ice is called pack ice.

Sometimes, the pack ice jams together and blocks ships from passing through. Then super-strong ships called icebreakers are needed to break a path through the pack ice.

What if the Ice Melted?

If all the ice on Earth melted, the sea level would rise by about six metres. If there was another ice age, more water would freeze and the sea level would fall.

At the moment, sea levels are rising at about three millimetres every year. This is believed to be because of the warming of the Earth's climate. Melting ice and rising sea levels also affect areas far away from the frozen regions.

Many islands in the Pacific Ocean are low lying. Rising sea levels threaten to cover some of them in a few hundred years.

Glossary

drone — A remote controlled aircraft

glacier — A slow-moving river of ice

ice age — A time in the past when ice covered a large part of the Earth's surface

ice cap — An area of permanent ice

ice shelf — A thick sheet of floating ice that has been pushed out into the ocean by a glacier

ice sheet — An area of ice that covers a large area, such as Antarctica where the ice sheet covers five and a half million square miles

iceberg — A large block of ice that has broken off from an ice shelf

pack ice — Floating sea ice that forms in the winter

Index

Arctic 3, 4–5, 8
Antarctica 3, 6–7, 8, 9, 12, 14
B15 iceberg 12–13
Emperor penguins 7
fresh water 19
glaciers 8
Ice Age 2
icebergs 10–19
icebreakers 16, 21
ice shelves 9
Inuit people 5
Lapp people 5
pack ice 20–21
Ross Ice Shelf 9
Titanic 15